DISNEY · PIXAR

Learn to Draw

TOY STORY

COLLECTOR'S EDITION

Walter Foster Jr.

Printed in China
1 3 5 7 9 10 8 6 4 2

Learn to Draw

Disney · PIXAR

TOY STORY

COLLECTOR'S EDITION

Table of Contents

How to Use This Book

Just follow these simple steps, and you'll be amazed at how fun and easy drawing can be!

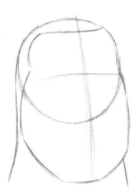

1 Draw the basic shape of the character; then add simple guidelines to help you place the features.

2 Each new step is shown in blue. Simply follow the blue lines to add the details.

3 Erase any lines you don't want to keep.

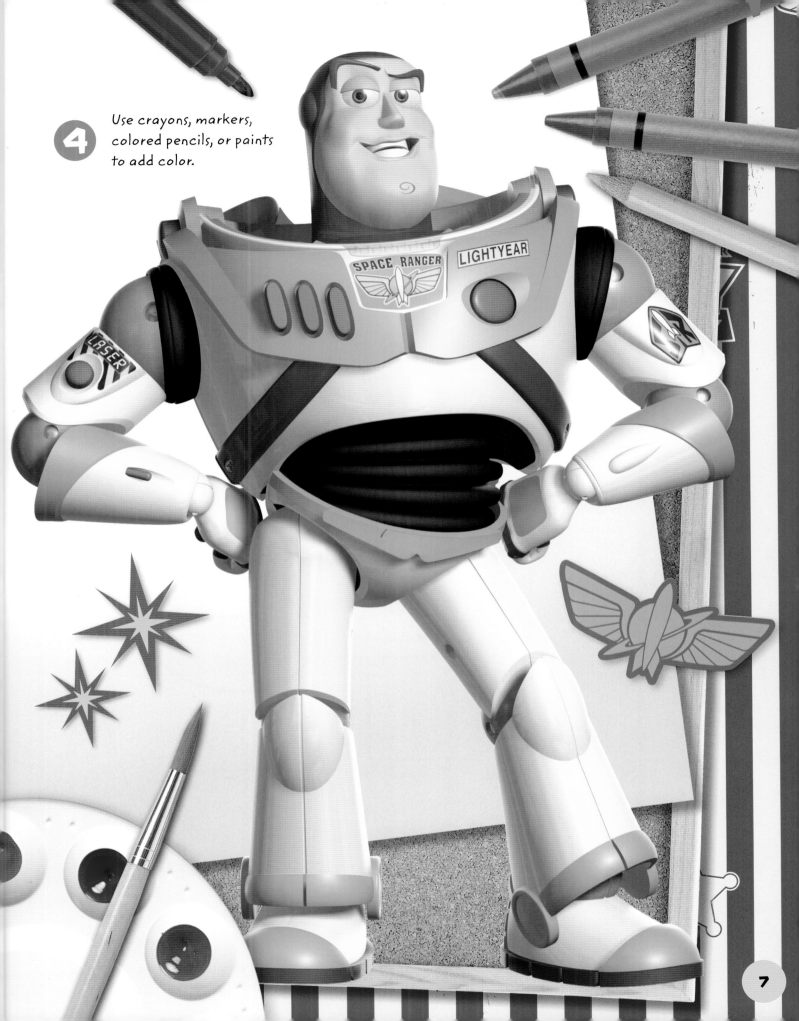

4 Use crayons, markers, colored pencils, or paints to add color.

Drawing Exercises

Warm up your hand by drawing lots of squiggles and shapes.

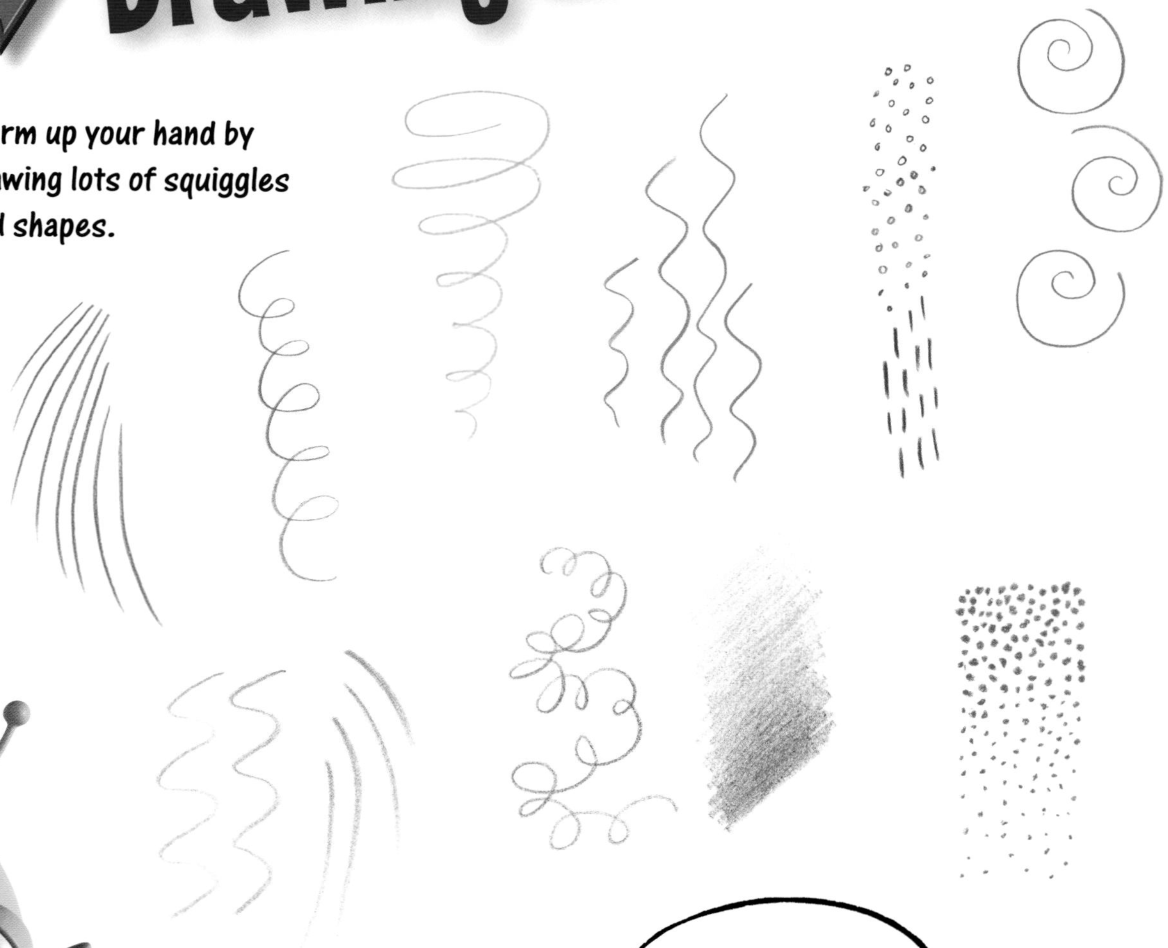

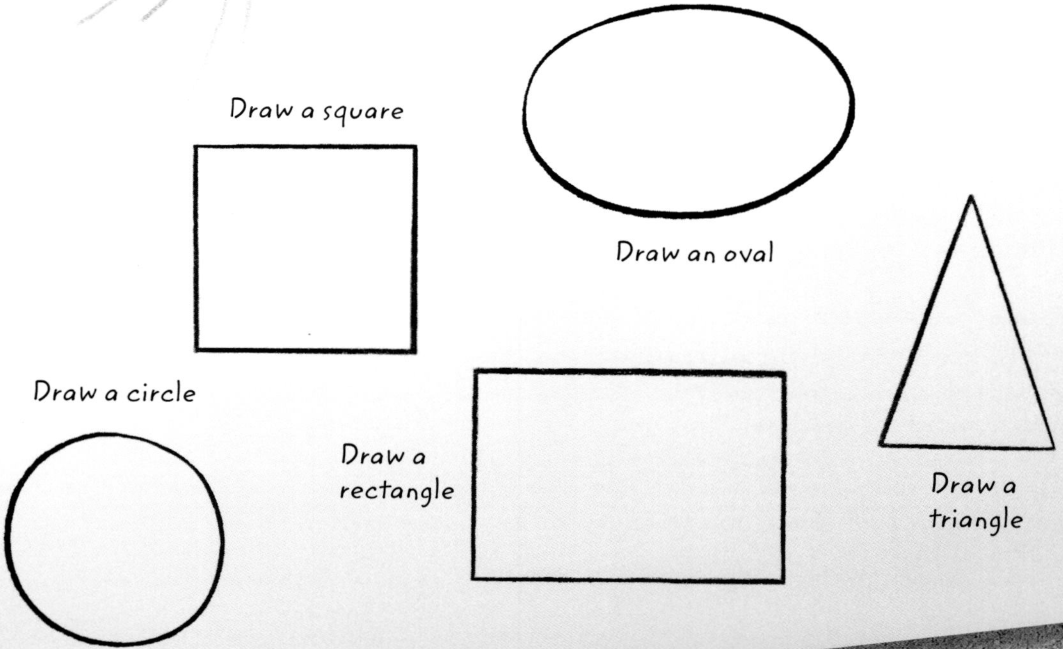

Draw a square

Draw an oval

Draw a circle

Draw a rectangle

Draw a triangle

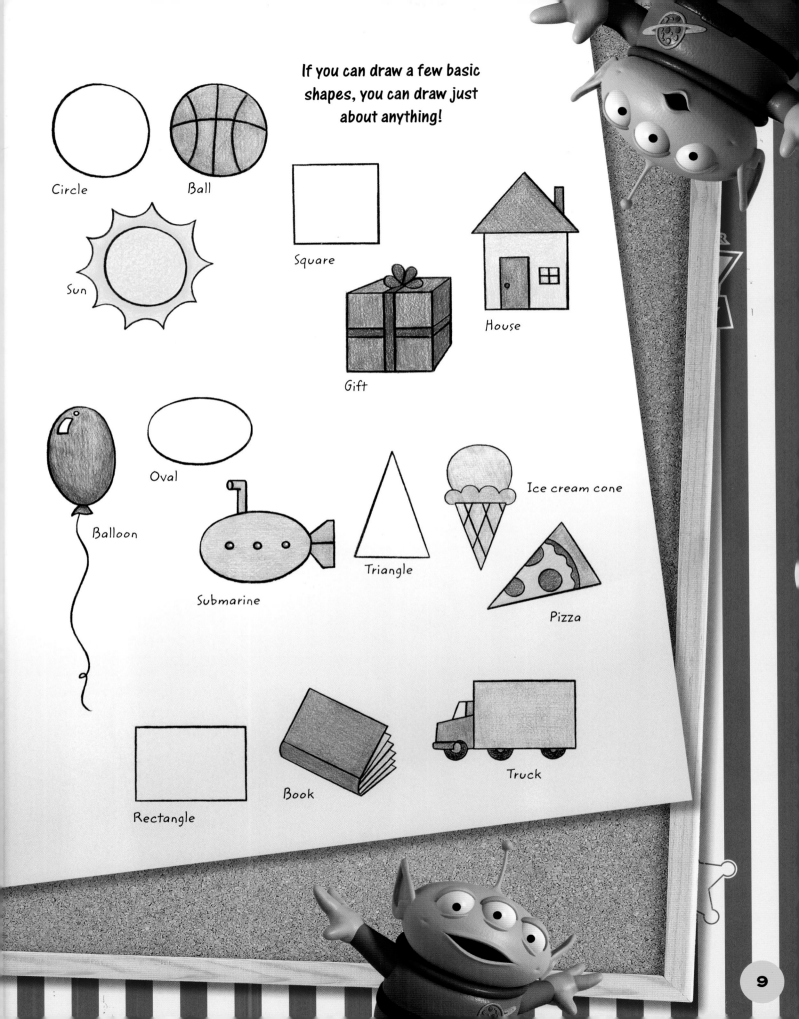

If you can draw a few basic shapes, you can draw just about anything!

Circle

Ball

Sun

Square

Gift

House

Balloon

Oval

Submarine

Triangle

Ice cream cone

Pizza

Rectangle

Book

Truck

WOODY

Woody, a talking sheriff doll with a pull string, was top toy in Andy's room. That was a tough spot to share with the new toy Buzz Lightyear, who thought he was a real space ranger. But Woody has learned how to share the limelight with friends, both old and new. After their owner Andy grows up and is off to college, Woody and his friends have a new home with the energetic and imaginative Bonnie. Bonnie's toys have welcomed the gang with open arms, but transitioning to a new owner after so many years is harder than Woody had thought it would be.

1

2

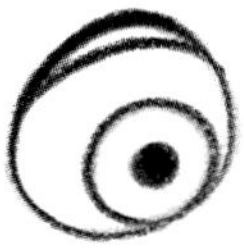

round eyes,
large iris

ears are flat
on top

3

FROM THE
HIT SHOW!

PULL-STRING
ACTION!

8 PHRASES!

4

YES!
teeth are one long
rectangle

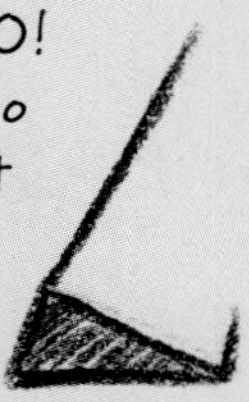

NO!

5

YES!

NO!
too
straight

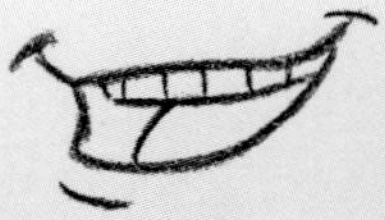

1

forearms are longer than upper arms

calves are longer than thighs

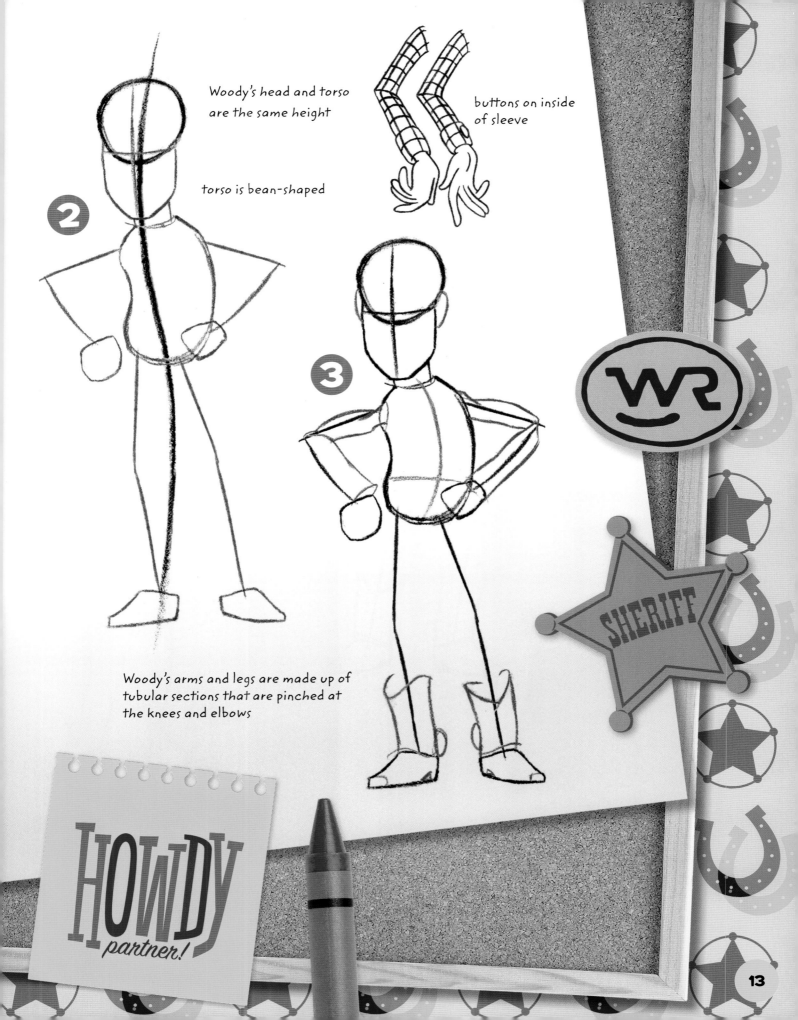

Woody's head and torso are the same height

buttons on inside of sleeve

torso is bean-shaped

2

3

Woody's arms and legs are made up of tubular sections that are pinched at the knees and elbows

WR

SHERIFF

HOWDY partner!

4

5

hat fits squarely on head

bandana accents silhouette

Let's RIDE!

⑥

sheriff badge
is a 5-point star

Woody
is about
4 heads
tall

15

HOWDY
partner!

⑦

top view of
Woody's hat

there is
stitching
around the
edges

hat band comes up 1/4 of
hat height

8 pointed
spurs

⑧

Let's
RIDE!

buckle has a
steer-head
design

WR

BUZZ LIGHTYEAR

When Buzz Lightyear, Space Ranger, first joined the toys in Andy's room, he didn't understand that he was a toy. But Buzz learned his lesson well and sometimes has to remind Woody of what it means to be a toy! Transitioning from living with Andy to their new owner Bonnie was a big change, but Buzz has taken the move in stride. Though no longer the toy of the moment, Buzz is as bold and trustworthy as ever, always ready for a new adventure.

Buzz's chin takes up about 1/3 of his head

1

2

the chin cleft is 1/2 the distance between lower lip and chin

18

eyes can change shape in exaggerated expressions

3

chin cleft looks like the number 9

4

iris is about ⅓ the size of the eye

YES!   NO!

brow should barely touch eye in normal pose; keep brows thick

5

full wingspan
is about 3
shoulder widths

1

angled

straight

2

3

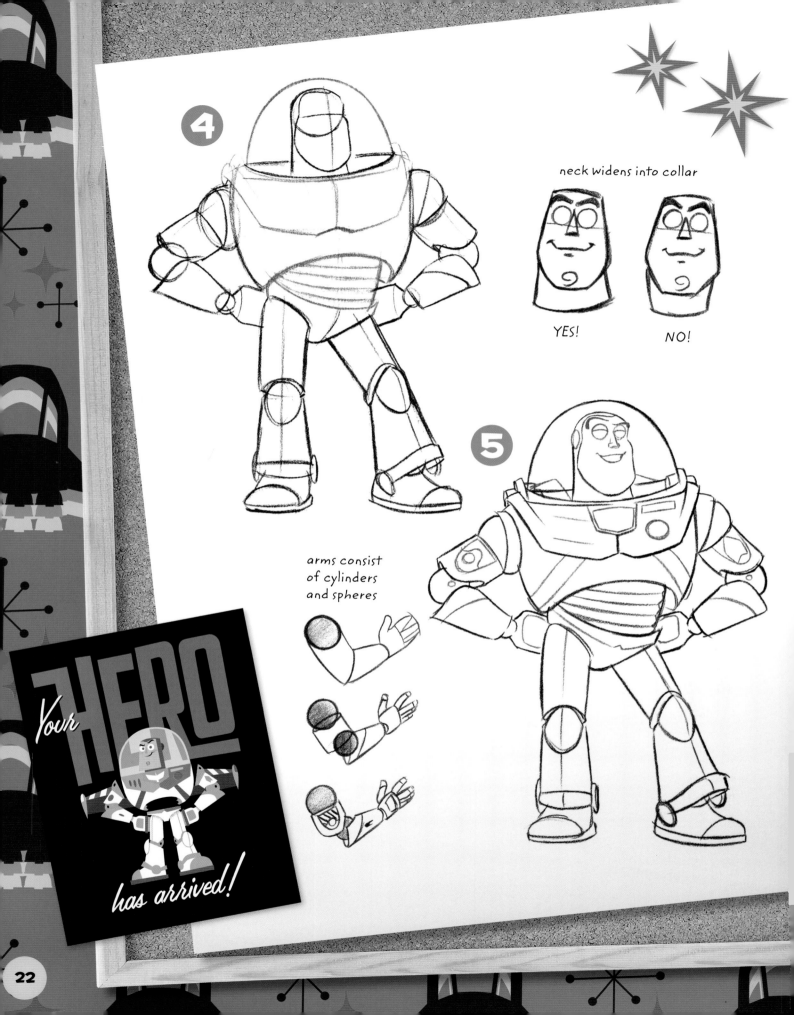

4

neck widens into collar

YES!   NO!

5

arms consist of cylinders and spheres

Your HERO has arrived!

fingers are tubular

6

basic shape of
backpack is like a
turtle's shell

ACTION
FIGURE

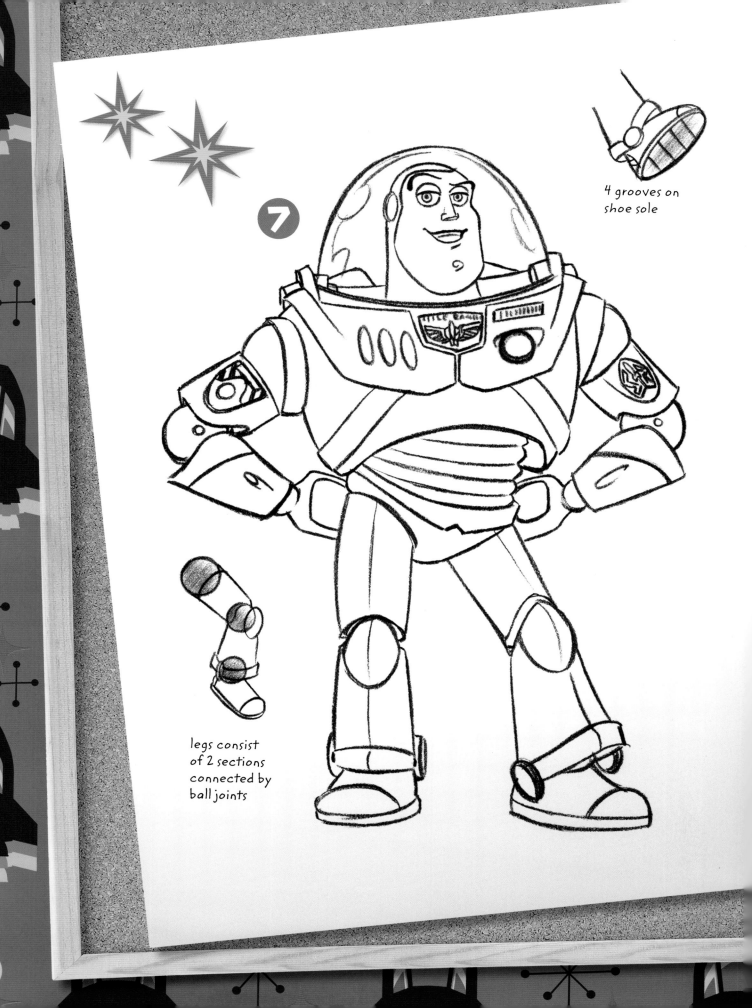

7

4 grooves on shoe sole

legs consist of 2 sections connected by ball joints

ACTION
FIGURE

8

SPACE RANGER   LIGHTYEAR

LASER

Your HERO

has arrived!

25

BULLSEYE

Bullseye, the sharpest horse in the West, is a trusty, energetic steed that loves Woody more than anything else in the world. This proud pony would do almost anything to keep his favorite sheriff out of harm's way.

1

3 locks go forward

4½ locks go down like a saw blade

mouth low on muzzle

SHERIFF

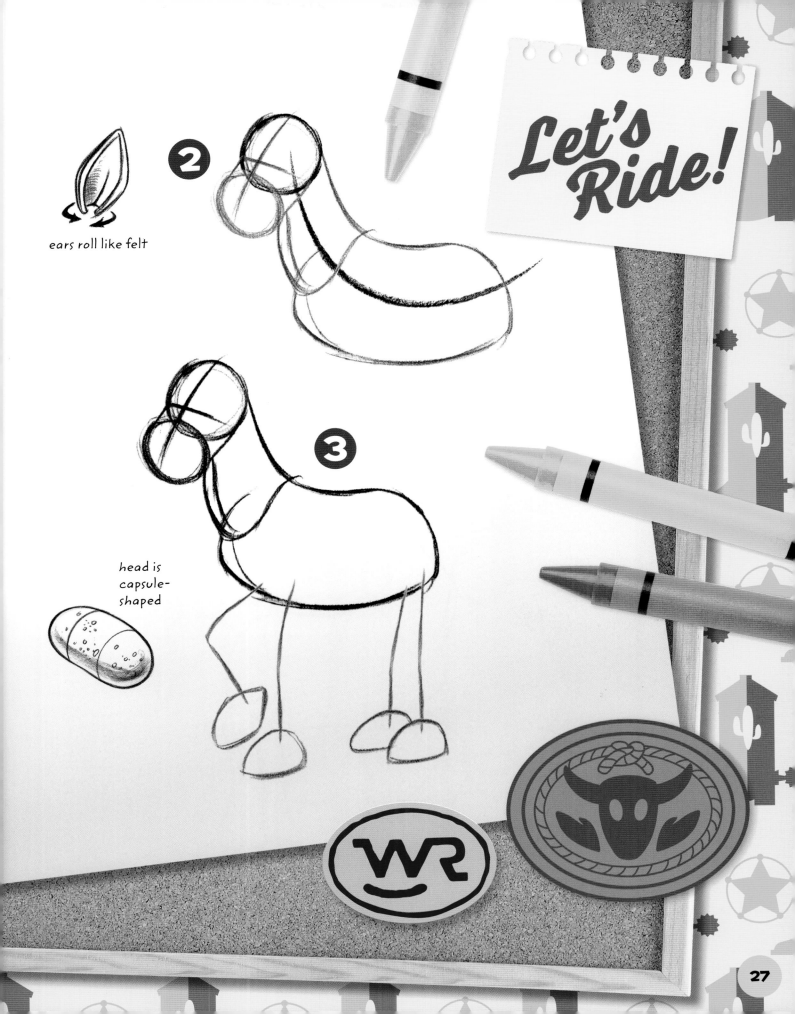

ears roll like felt

2

head is
capsule-
shaped

3

Let's Ride!

bottom points of
tail line up

4

5

SHERIFF

try to keep a
clear line of
action

6

Let's Ride!

legs are loose and floppy

7

bottom of hoof is shaped like an upside-down U

YES!
eyes slant
apart slightly

8

NO! not too much

legs are 2
stuffed sections,
almost shaped
like peanuts

REX

This toy dinosaur is one nervous Rex. When he's not worried about being replaced by a bigger dino toy, he's trying to avoid conflict in Andy's room. Rex's growl "almost" scares the other toys.

head is block-shaped

legs attach high on lower body

1

"yikes!"

make sure upper body flows smoothly from spherical lower body

2

cone-shaped teeth

3

FEAR ME! (PLEASE!)

Rex's pupils are tiny

FEAR ME! (PLEASE!)

4

5

keep equal distance
between toenails

6

"the sky is falling!"

legs are thick

7

torso is pear shaped

tiny arms with clawed fingers

Mr. Potato Head

Mr. Potato Head can be cranky sometimes, but he's always there when Mrs. Potato Head needs another spud to lean on.

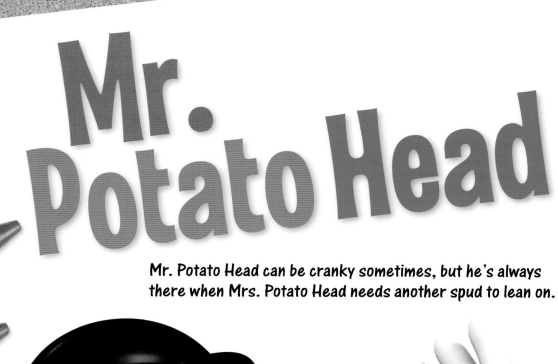

large oval-shaped eyes

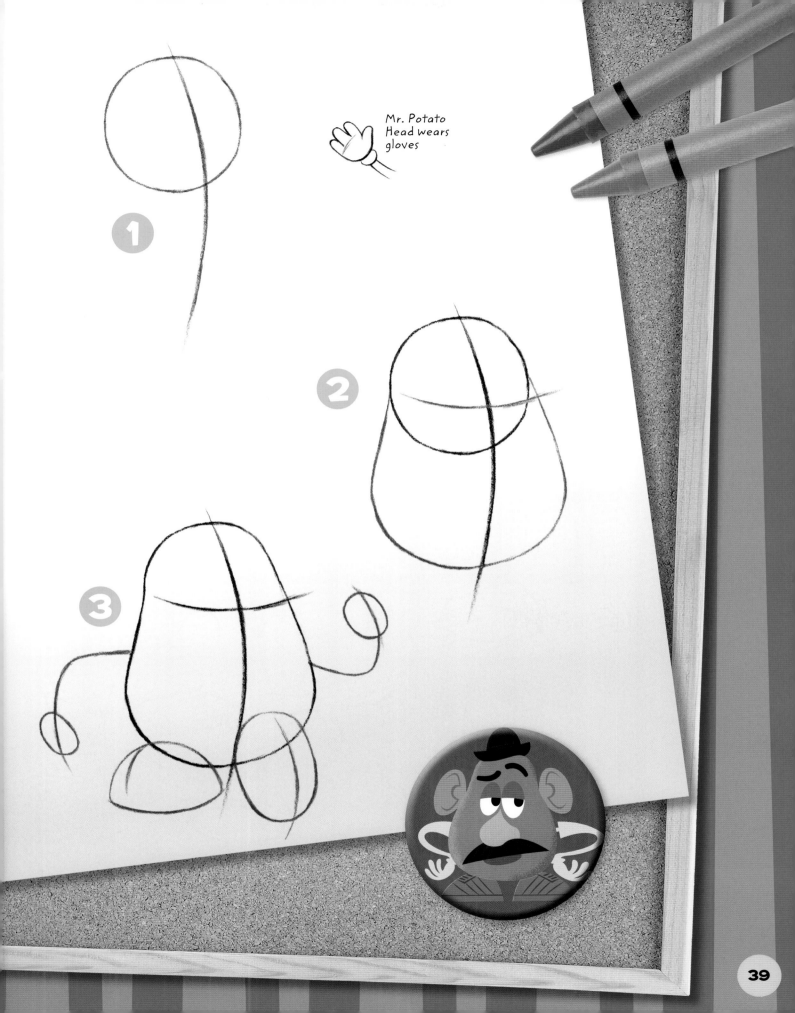

Mr. Potato
Head wears
gloves

1

2

3

4

5

6

mustache
curves down   YES!

NO!

HAMM

You can always count on Hamm to put in his two cents on any topic. As Andy's piggy bank and Mr. Potato Head's buddy (spuddy?), Hamm says what he thinks...especially when he thinks Woody's headed for trouble.

mouth is a small slit on bottom of snout

1

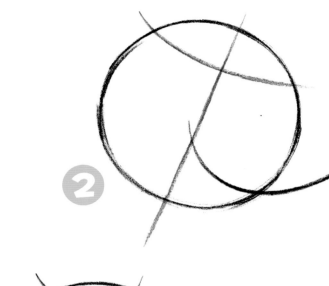

2

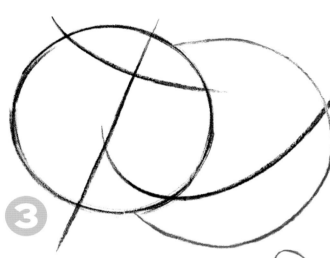

3

It's time for
¢HANGE
YA!

3 toes

small ears

4

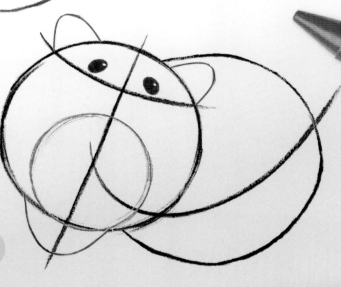

START $AVING TODAY!
THE ORIGINAL PLASTIC PIGGY BANK

eyes are high on head

nostrils lie on top of halfway line on nose

small bottom teeth

nose fits on head like a cup on a sphere

Hamm's coin slot

5

6

eyes can squash and stretch depending on expression

don't forget his tail and cork!

pear-shaped body

It's time for CHANGE YA!

JESSIE

Jessie knows what it means to be a toy. She once belonged to a little girl who loved her as much as Andy loves Woody. But after that little girl gave Jessie away, the brokenhearted cowgirl decided that being a collectible is better than being with a child who might outgrow you. Woody has to remind Jessie what being a toy is all about.

Jessie's body is flexible like a rag doll's

TOUGH cookie

1

2

3 fringe pieces

stitching wraps
around cuff

her hat usually sits on the back of her head

③

④

TOUGH

cookie

FROM THE HIT TELEVISION SHOW!

8

don't forget her ponytail

Woody's hat is triangular

Jessie's hat is rounder

THE PROSPECTOR

The Prospector may seem like a nice, grandfatherly type of fellow at first, but when his true feelings are revealed, it becomes clear that he's just plain selfish and mean. Having never belonged to a child, the Prospector simply doesn't know how to play—or be loved.

mustache changes with mood

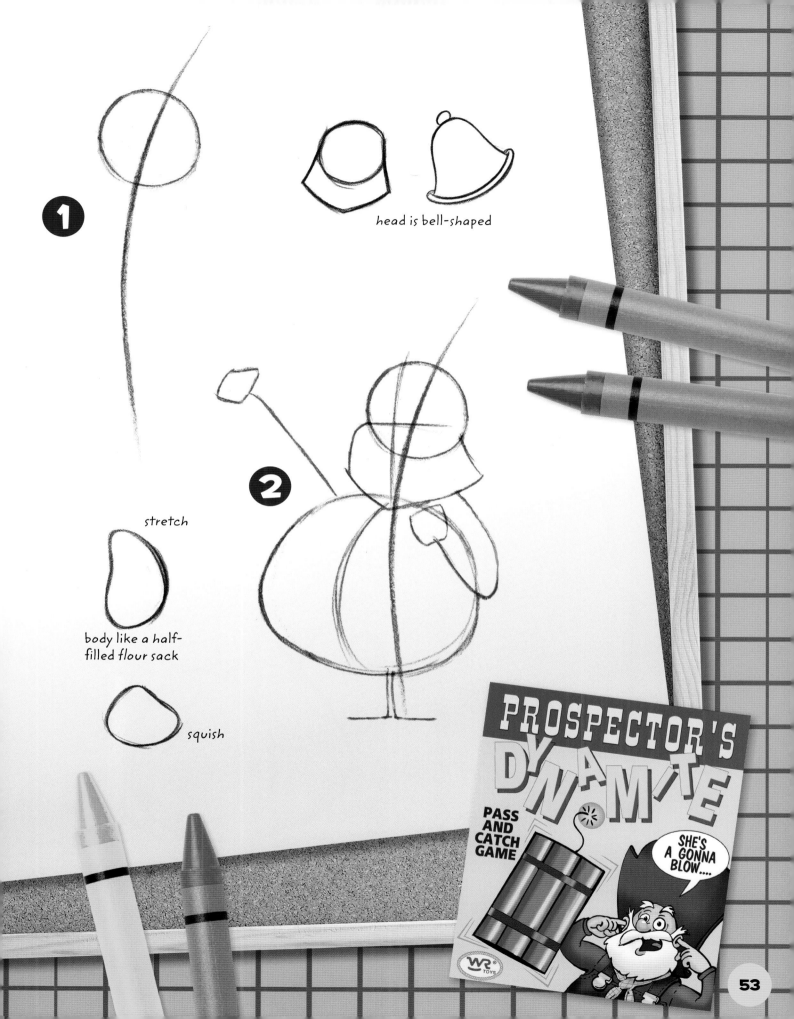

1

head is bell-shaped

2

stretch

body like a half-filled flour sack

squish

PROSPECTOR'S DYNAMITE

PASS AND CATCH GAME

SHE'S A GONNA BLOW....

WR TOYS

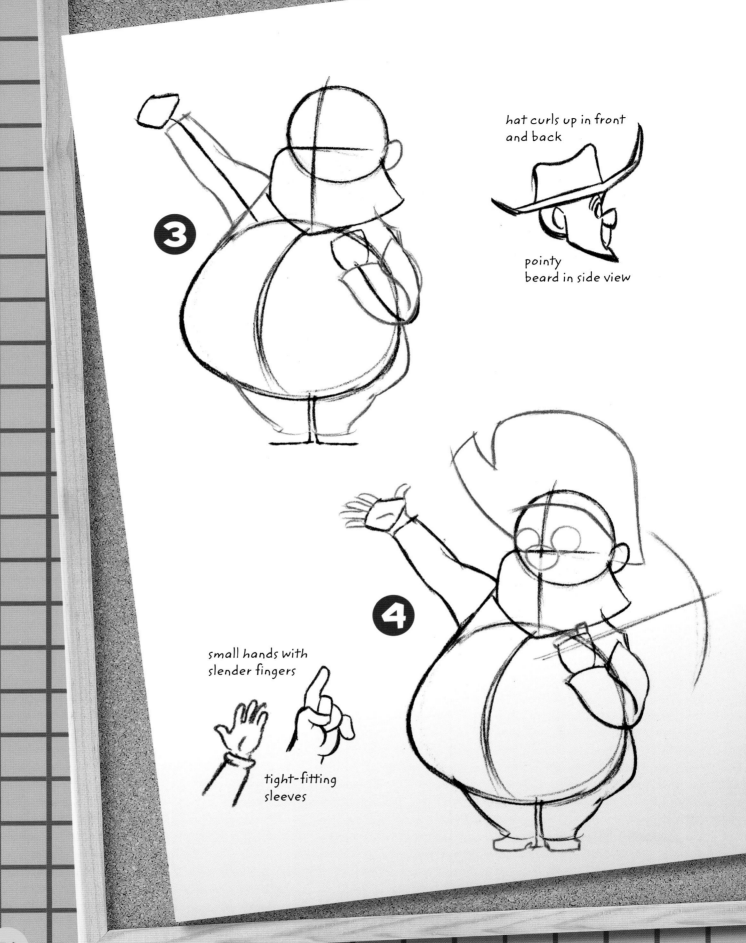

hat curls up in front
and back

pointy
beard in side view

3

4

small hands with
slender fingers

tight-fitting
sleeves

5

relaxed gesture

excited gesture

PROSPECTOR'S DYNAMITE

PASS AND CATCH GAME

SHE'S A GONNA BLOW....

6

the Prospector is
never without his
pickaxe

7

boot flares
at top

Slinky Dog

"Slink" always has a spring in his step. He's a happy-go-lucky toy dog and one of Woody's strongest supporters. When Woody needs help, Slinky Dog goes the extra mile—or at least as far as his spring will stretch.

spring compresses and shortens body

①

Slinky is a pull toy, so he has a wheel on each foot

back legs have
bendable knees

Watch Me Stretch!

body is 2 halves of a sphere
attached with a spring

eye lies halfway
up on head circle

7

thick, heavy brows

round eyes

head is a ball

8

Aliens

It's a small world for the Alien toys at Pizza Planet. They live to see whom "the Claw" will pluck from their crane-game world. While trapped inside the crane game, the Aliens obey the Claw's calling, but once they leave, they happily switch their loyalty to others—like Mr. Potato Head, much to his chagrin.

1

5

6

7

8

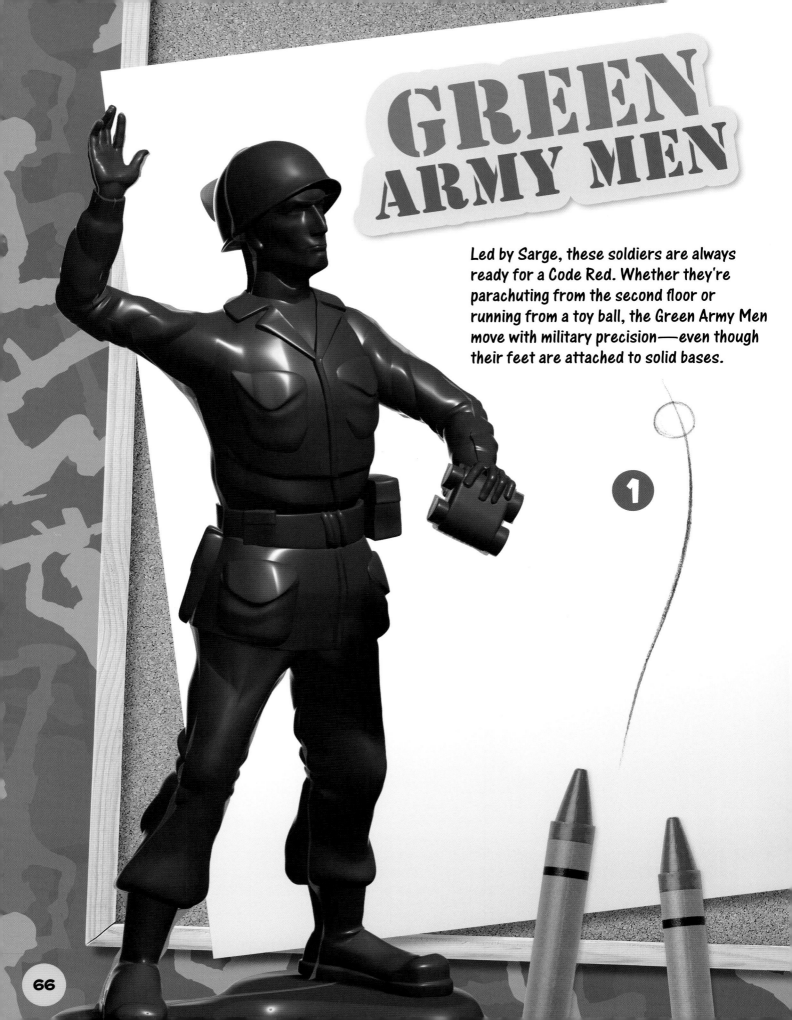

GREEN ARMY MEN

Led by Sarge, these soldiers are always ready for a Code Red. Whether they're parachuting from the second floor or running from a toy ball, the Green Army Men move with military precision—even though their feet are attached to solid bases.

1

ZURG

The Universe—and Al's Toy Barn—is not a safe place with the evil Emperor Zurg on the loose. Zurg is smart enough to escape from the store and strong enough to take on Buzz and New Buzz, but he's unlucky enough to be on the receiving end of Rex's swinging tail.

evil Z shape on cape clasp

cape can flow for dramatic effect

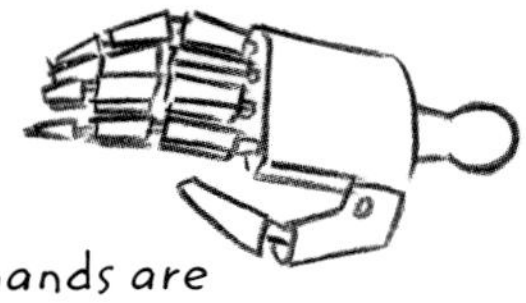

1

**hands are
composed of sharp
steel parts with
claw-like fingers**

2

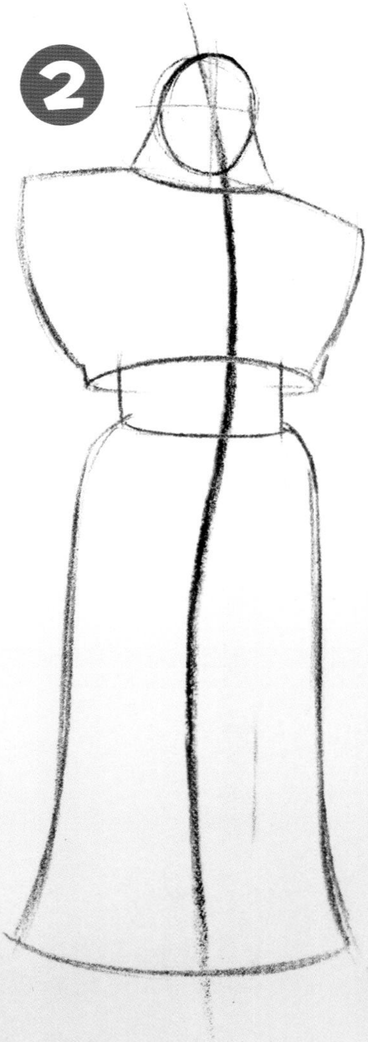

**fingers
resemble
armor plates**

3

head composed
of many
triangular
shapes

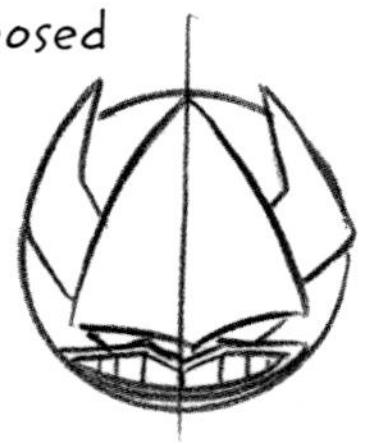

4

concave   convex

Zurg's   Buzz's
gauntlet   gauntlet

5

5 torso rings

angle of horns is
about 45 degrees

YES!

NO!

NO!

6

7

visor appears
triangular in
all views

8 glowing yellow teeth

"feet" are 3
wheels

LOTSO

Lots-o'-Huggin' Bear—a.k.a Lotso—seems like nothing more than the nicest teddy bear at Sunnyside Daycare. But Lotso's true colors are exposed when he traps Andy's toys in the Caterpillar Room with all of the rambunctious toddlers— and later when he leaves the toys to be incinerated at the garbage dump.

ears are 2 half circles

1

2

eyebrows are
wide and bushy

YES!

NO!

I'M A
HUGGER

I'M A HUGGER

3

his cane is
a wooden
mallet

4

5

eyes are round
and set close
together

nose is an
upside-down
rounded
triangle

6

7

I'M A
HUGGER

8

teardrop-
shaped paws

BIG BABY

Big Baby (along with Lotso and Chuckles) was accidentally left at a rest stop by his first owner, Daisy. Although Big Baby initially does Lotso's dirty work at Sunnyside Daycare, once he realizes how much he misses his mama, he helps the toys escape from Lotso's grasp.

1

full lips   YES!

NO!

5

6

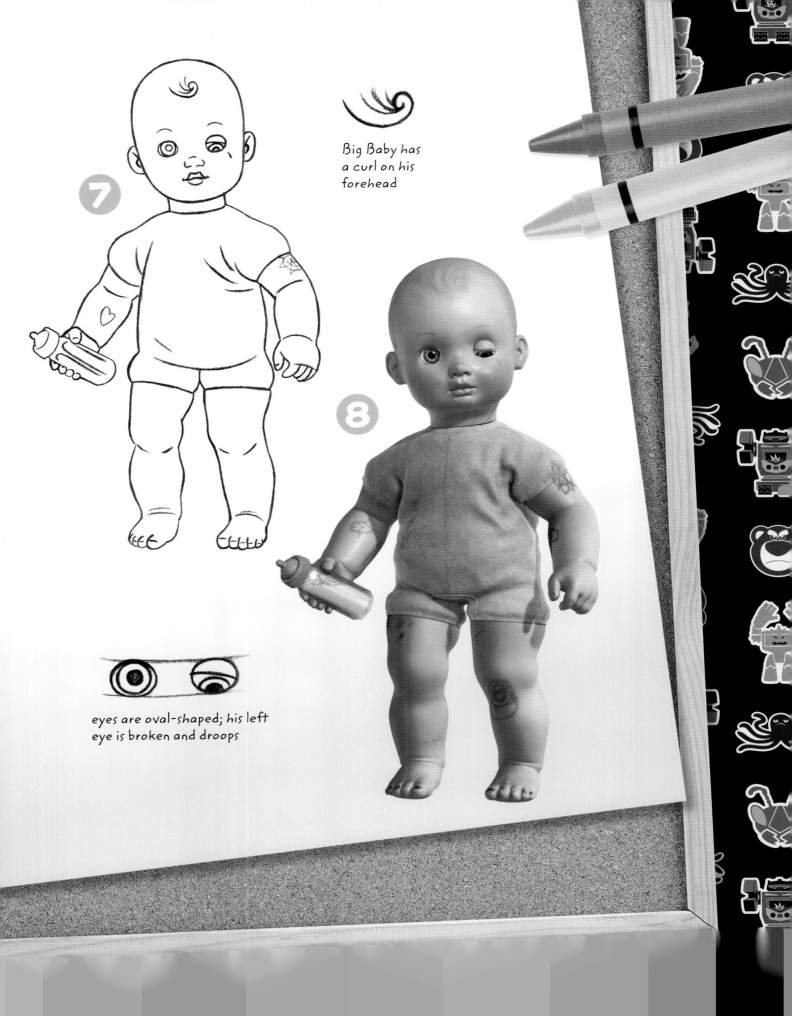

7

Big Baby has
a curl on his
forehead

8

eyes are oval-shaped; his left
eye is broken and droops

CHUNK

Another of Lotso's cronies at Sunnyside Daycare, Chunk is a two-faced plastic rock monster who goes from friendly to foul with the punch of a button.

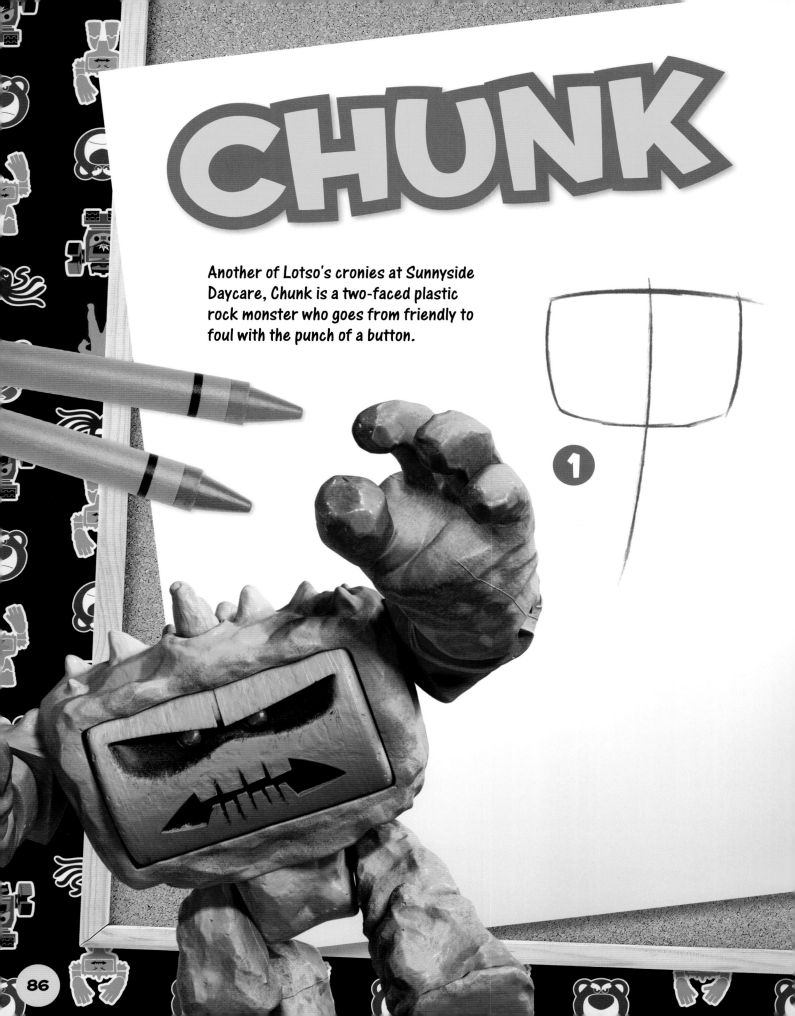

1

5

Chunk has two faces

6

Mr. Pricklepants

Mr. Pricklepants is no ordinary hedgehog. This lederhosen-wearing toy is both dramatic and intellectual. He is also very kind to all of the other toys in Bonnie's toy collection.

Mr. Pricklepants is about $^1/_2$ Woody's size

1

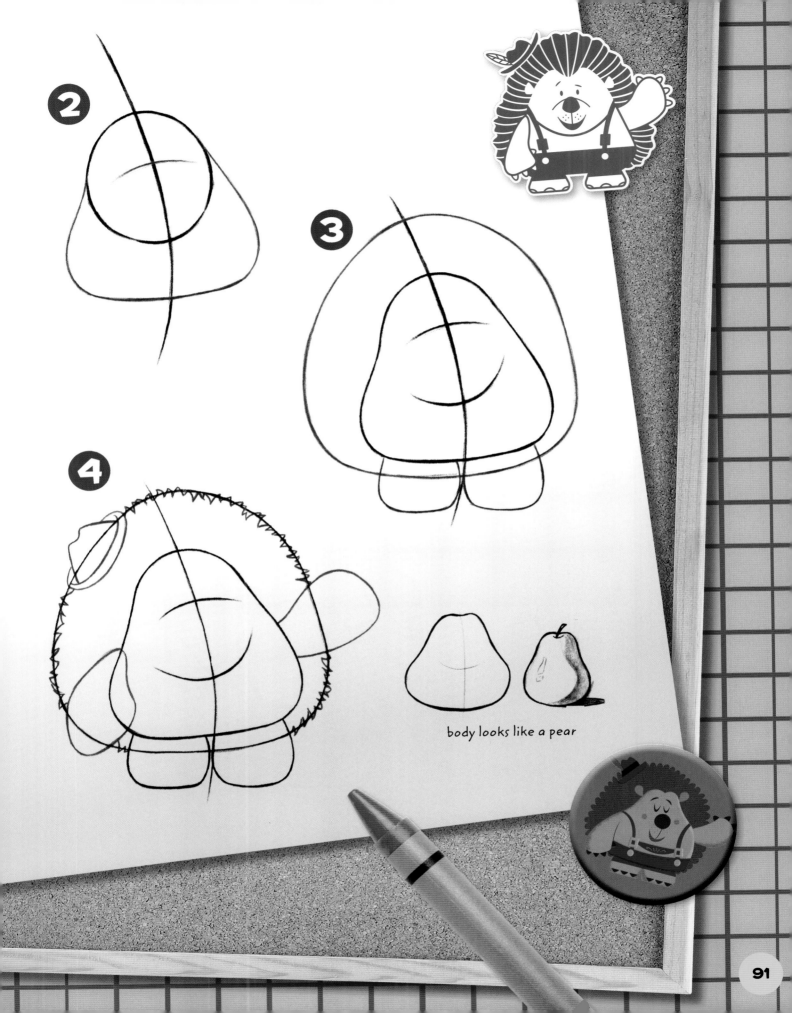

body looks like a pear

5

hat looks like an
upside-down cup
on a saucer

claws
are small
triangles

arms taper

6

7

8

suspenders
have a
buckle

Buttercup

Buttercup may look like a cute and cuddly unicorn, but he's really a gruff, no-nonsense member of Bonnie's toy collection.

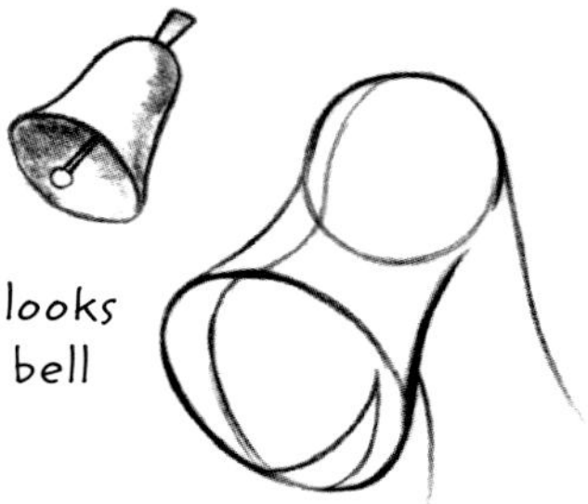

head looks like a bell

1

2

horn has 5 parts

tail is short
and bushy

eyes are ovals, pupils and irises are round, and his eyebrows follow the shape of eye

body is drawn from simple shapes

8

7

nostrils
are heart-
shaped

BO PEEP

Bo Peep is a porcelain figurine who, along with her sheep, Billy, Goat, and Gruff, once decorated the base of a child's reading lamp. Don't let her delicate appearance fool you—Bo is as brave and tough as they come, with a dry sense of humor and lightning-quick reflexes. After Andy's sister, Molly, outgrew the lamp and gave it away, Bo and her sheep became "lost toys" by choice, traveling from town to town and helping others they meet along the way.

5

FORKY

Forky is a craft project created by Bonnie on the first day of kindergarten from a spork and art supplies. After being played with and coming to life, Forky has a lot of questions about his new existence as a toy.

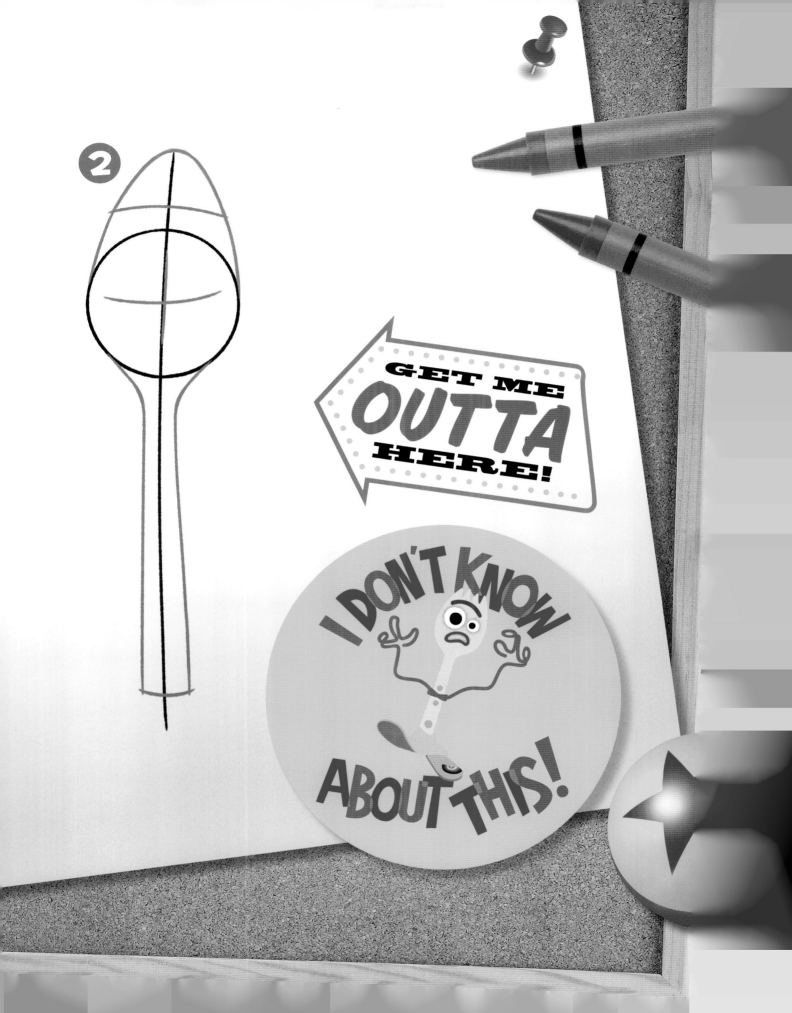

I DON'T KNOW ABOUT THIS!

DUKE CABOOM

Duke Caboom has all the swagger of Canada's greatest daredevil, but he's never quite recovered from being discarded by his kid after Duke's stunt cycle jumps turned out not to be as cool as advertised.

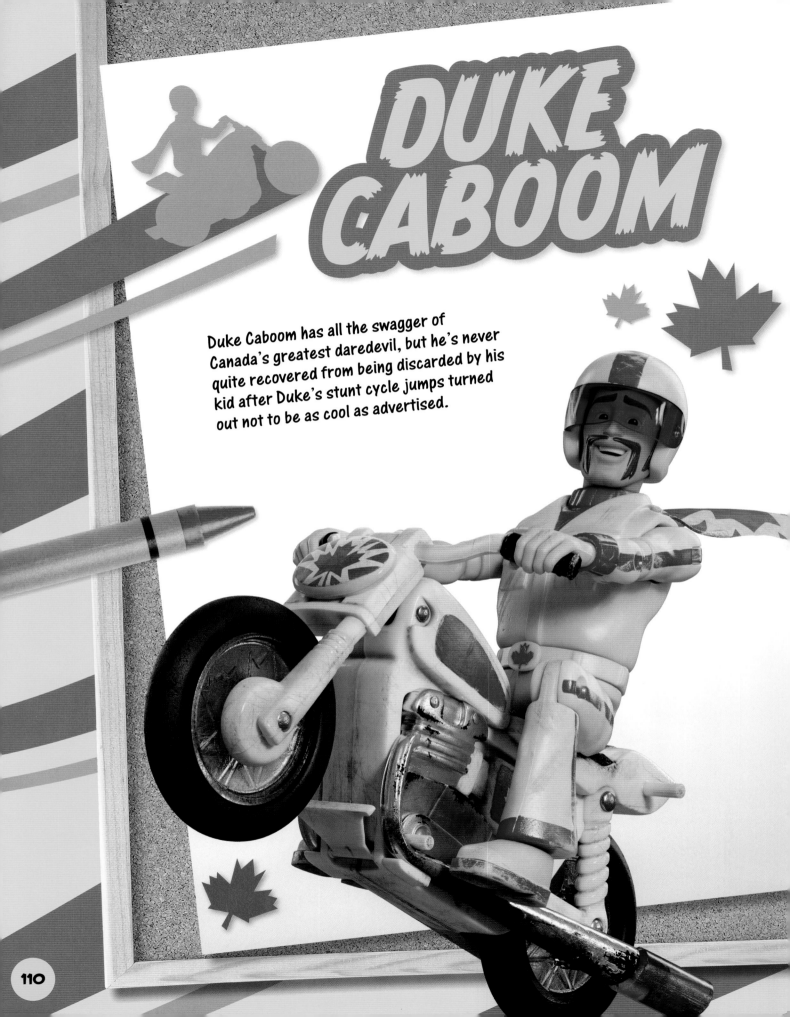

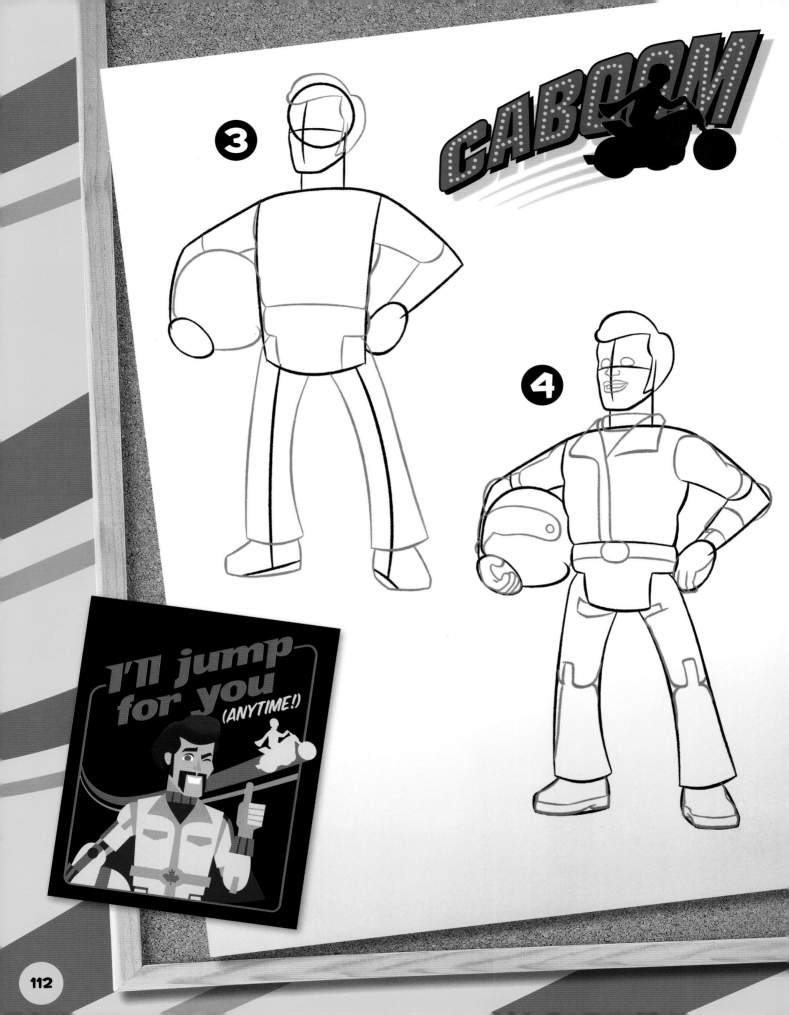

3

4

CABOOM!

I'll jump for you (ANYTIME!)

I'll jump
for you
(ANYTIME!)

DUCKY & BUNNY

Ducky and Bunny are a pair of carnival-prize stuffed toys who are literally inseparable. They are attached to one another by their wing and paw. After hanging in a carnival game for years waiting to be won, their senses of humor are as sharp as ever.

You're
STUCK
with us!

STICK with US!

Gabby

Talking doll Gabby Gabby looks straight out of her original ads from the 1950s, but for some reason she's spent decades languishing in the glass display cabinet of an antiques store.

me

me

Queen of
GAB

ALSO AVAILABLE FROM WALTER FOSTER JR.

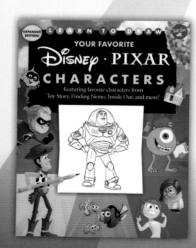
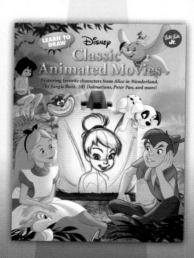